THE
IMPRESSIONS OF SAN FRANCISCO
ADVANCED ASSISTANT SERIES
VOLUME 1:
TREATMENT ACCEPTANCE

9 781300 434641
ISBN 978-1-300-43464-1

THE IMPRESSIONS OF SAN FRANCISCO ADVANCED ASSISTANT SERIES VOLUME 1: TREATMENT ACCEPTANCE

For Dental Assistants Who Would Like to Become More Valuable Team Members by Learning How to Contribute to the Financial Success of the Dental Practice

Jen Green, RDA

For my husband Dave,
For my Mom and Dad
For my favorite dentist, Sean
and
For business-savvy dental assistants everywhere

PREFACE

I've been working on this project off and on over the last year or so, not being able to decide whether to turn the project into a book or to just submit it as an article. It seemed too short for a book but too long for an article so I had the idea to simply create little volumes of all the topics I'd like to share with dental assistants; this is the first. I teach several different continuing education courses and many of them are geared toward dental assistants. While hands-on skills like taking perfect impressions and creating beautiful provisional restorations are important, they're not enough to make a dental assistant an indispensible employee. As a dental assistant, I took really great impressions and awesome photos and my temporaries weren't too shabby either, but the role I played in treatment acceptance is what really made me stand out. As an educator, it's always been my goal to help dental assistants to become more valuable in the workplace and I'm hoping that this book will inspire you to set, meet and exceed goals that will help make you the most productive, irreplaceable team member in the office.

CONTENT

**TAKING AN ACTIVE ROLE IN
INCREASING PRACTICE PRODUCTION
Page 18**

- *Contributing to the financial success of the business*
- *Setting your own production goals*

**STORES ARE NEVER NICE TO PEOPLE;
THEY'RE NICE TO CREDIT CARDS.
Page 23**

- *Working with high-maintenance patients*
- *Knowing how your patients spend their money*

**IMPROVING DENTIST-ASSISTANT COMMUNICATION AND
WORKING TOGETHER TO REACH YOUR GOALS
Page 26**

- *Getting better results by communicating more effectively with your employer*

**BECOMING MORE KNOWLEDGEABLE ABOUT
HUMAN BEHAVIOR AND HOW WE MAKE DECISIONS
Page 28**

- *Understanding past experiences, bias and the escalation of commitment*

**BESIDES WHAT YOU SEE, I HAVE CONFIDENCE IN ME!
Page 31**

- *Gaining the confidence you need to get the results you want*
- *How continuing education can improve your confidence*

CONCLUSION
Page 33

- *Review of topics covered and planning tools to implement the skills learned*
- *Planning tools to help you get started*

THE DENTAL ASSISTANT'S ROLE
IN TREATMENT ACCEPTANCE

I'm not sure if he was the original person to come up with the patient communication version of the BLT acronym, but I first heard it from a Dallas-area dentist about ten years ago. He said that before patients will accept and move forward with a treatment plan, they have to *Believe* you, they have to *Like* you and they have to *Trust* you. He said, "Give 'em a BLT!" and I'll always remember that because I think it's true. People do need to believe, like and trust those with whom they do business.

In clinical dentistry we are caregivers, but it is in fact a business. Sure, your office may have a certain philosophy or mission statement about how you care for your patients, but the success of the business will be dependent upon its ability to consistently make money. Some of it will be "easy money" in the form of fees collected for preventative procedures- what the patient needs. Patients have already been trained to know that they need cleanings, x-rays and periodontal charting. They know that if they don't get a cavity filled they might need a root canal in the future. The dental IQ of patients is much higher than it was when I entered the field in 1994. This can probably be attributed to the discussion of dentistry on TV, radio, magazines, Facebook, Yelp and other forms of media. Patients' dental IQs have gone up, just as the way we receive information has become more sophisticated. I think this is a good thing because it has helped create value for what we do. Creating value in the mind of the patient is right up there with giving them a "BLT". It has to happen before the patient will move forward with treatment.

WHY THE DENTAL ASSISTANT IS IMPORTANT
IN TREATMENT ACCEPTANCE

We are caregivers but dentistry is in fact a business, the way your employer makes a living, and in some cases provides for a family. While the entire team is tasked with ensuring the success of the business, the dental assistant has the best chance of bonding with the patients- and I'm not talking about adhesive dentistry! From a patient perspective, the dentist gets the money, the office manager takes the money, the hygienist might have a homecare lecture waiting for you and the dental assistant is the friendly person, the listener, the trusted one you make eye contact with when you need reassurance, your hand held, or a question answered when you're too intimidated to ask the dentist. As the dental assistant, you have the greatest opportunity to develop a relationship with the patient. While I think many hygienists do a great job of chatting it up with the patients, the majority of those appointments are spent with their hands in the patient's mouth. The dentist, though probably a pleasant well-liked person, needs to first concentrate on the patient's care. She benefits from having that right-hand person there to make conversation and keep the patient at ease while freeing the doctor's mind to devote all thoughts and energy to the task at hand.

I'VE GOT TO HAND IT TO YOU

Yep, we've been handing stuff to dentists forever, it seems. But that's not all. We work our butts off doing all kinds of things- impressions, x-rays, provisional crowns and pouring models to name just a few. Creating your role in treatment acceptance is just adding to your repertoire. Any new addition can be a challenge and may seem really difficult at first. Think back to when you first entered the field. Some of us went to dental assisting school while others learned on-the-job. I went the classroom route and started in the dental assisting program at the local junior college in my hometown. It's funny to reflect on those days and how nervous I was about completing such simple tasks as setting up a restorative tray correctly or completing the sterilization process in the right order. I was so awkward. And terrified of starting my first intern assignment! It was a big deal to sit opposite the dentist for the first time and wipe excess who-knows-what off of their instrument. My hands were so clammy that they were slippery inside my gloves and my safety glasses were fogged as I sweated under my mask, willing myself not to drop anything. Then there was radiology lab where I'm proud to say it only took me about two hours to take an FMX. Ok, it might not have taken that long but it probably seemed like it to my poor volunteers! Hey, they're the ones who wanted free x-rays! Suckers! My coronal polish patients fared a little better with quick appointments and only a few fruity pumice splatters. Looking back, treatment acceptance is not really much different than the other skills I've learned. I had an awkward beginning, clammy hands, and I was still trying not to drop anything... like the ball!

CREATING VALUE

Most of my chairside experience is in comprehensive dentistry-the diagnosis, analysis, planning and treatment of a patient with equal consideration of their functional needs and cosmetic wants. It's not always the cosmetic aspect that needs the value-boost. Sometimes a patient has said "I want veneers." This is going to be easy, right? Maybe not. It could be that the patient has some bite interferences that will result in the destruction of any porcelain restorations placed. There are hundreds of dentists who would just give them the veneers they want, take the money and hope for the best. In comprehensive dentistry, we have to discipline ourselves to either do it the way we were trained or let the patient walk out the door and into someone else's office. Since the latter is not the desired result, we need to look at how we can create value so the patient will realize that they really do need to deal with the functional aspect of their care. To do this, you will first need to learn how to identify engineering problems and how to communicate them to a patient in their language- not the language we speak in "dental world". The more educated you are about it, the more effective your conversation with the patient will be. I'll label a few photos to give you some examples of both engineering and cosmetic issues, but first let's look at this veneer-seeking patient who has some bite issues to address.

How can we create value in this situation?
I'd probably say something like this:

"Here's a picture we took at your last visit. See how your teeth were already starting to look worn on the edges and cracks are starting to develop, especially here in front? If you take a look in this mirror, you can see that it's gotten worse since then and if we put veneers on your teeth now, the same thing could happen. We want your veneers to look great for you for a long time so the doctor will just need to make some adjustments to your bite first to help protect your investment in your new smile." *Image 1*

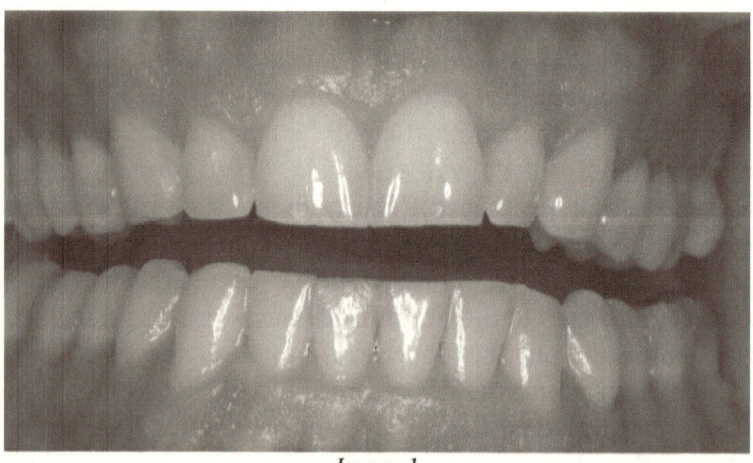

Image 1

WHAT TO SAY, WHEN TO SAY IT (AND WHEN TO SHUT UP)

When creating value for any type of treatment, try to give patients a non-dental explanation in a language they understand. Relating dental treatment to other ways they invest their money will help them make more educated decisions about how they spend it. This will also help to prevent them from changing their minds in the middle of a treatment phase because they didn't understand what was involved. Speak your individual patient's language. A good example for one patient may not be the right one for another. This is a good time for you to get creative and think of the best analogy you can use to help *this* patient understand why their treatment needs to be done in a certain way and in a particular order. Deliver your analogy, ending with an open-ended question (one that can't be answered with yes or no), then be quiet. Let the patient think about what you just said and wait for them to answer. The patient will answer when they're ready. It might be another question, but be quiet and wait for them to ask it. Give them time to think without interruption and continue the conversation when they're ready; not when you're ready to turn the room for the next patient.

People don't like to be rushed when making important decisions and treatment acceptance is an important decision. So this is a perfect time to remember when to shut up.

COMMUNICATING WITH PATIENTS ABOUT ENGINEERING ISSUES, SUCH AS WORN OR CRACKED TEETH

HERE ARE SOME EXAMPLES OF ENGINEERING ISSUES AS IDENTIFIED IN PATIENT PHOTOS:

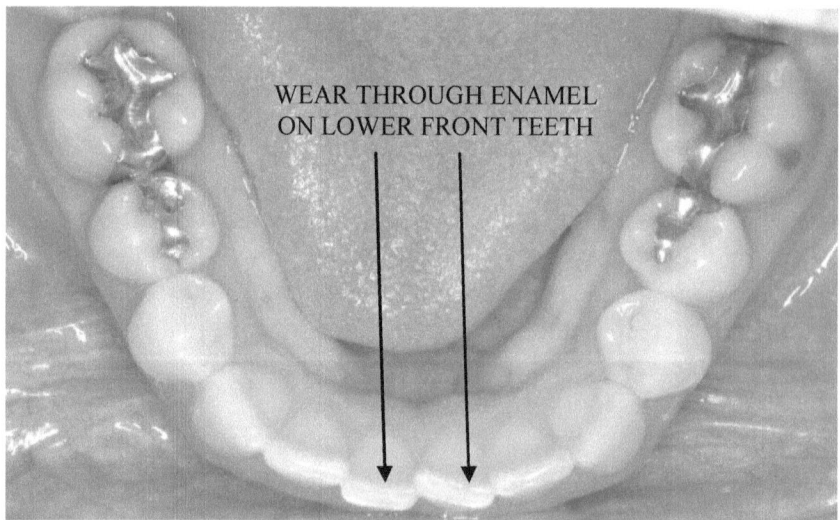

Image 2

Wear faceting is present on the lower anteriors, particularly on #24 and #25

Image 2

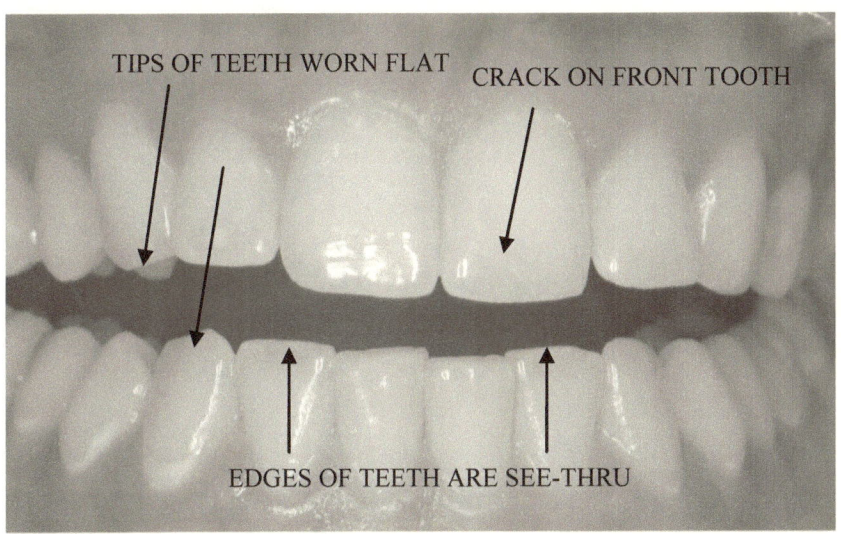

Image 3

The cuspids are flat, providing no anterior guidance. A craze line
runs from mesial to incisal of #9 and the edges of #23 and #26
are worn to the point of translucency. *Image 3*

TALKING WITH PATIENTS ABOUT COSMETIC DENTISTRY

EXAMPLES OF COSMETIC ISSUES:

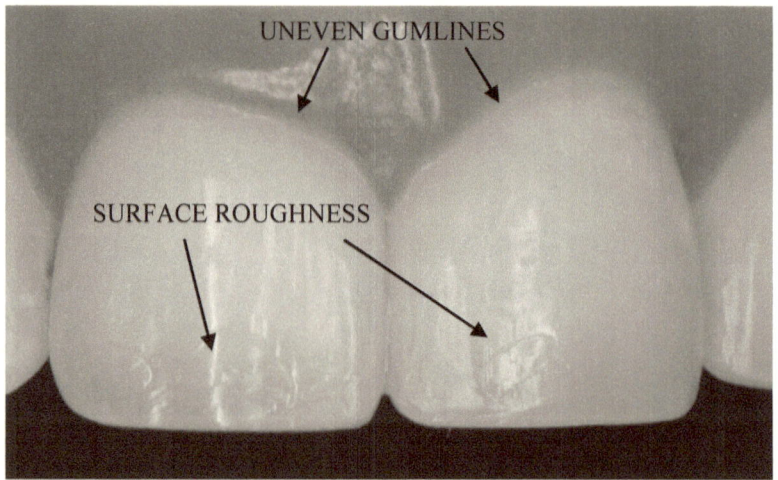

Image 4

Teeth #8 and #9 need gingival recontouring to create central symmetry. Facial sanding/polishing is needed to smooth rough surface, possibly from orthodontic bracket removal.

Image 4

VERBAL SKILLS TO HELP YOU CREATE VALUE
FOR SERVICES YOU OFFER

- QUESTION: "Why do I need a nightguard?"
- ANSWER: "The nightguard will help protect your investment in your veneers."
  (Drop the word "investment" whenever possible because patients know that an investment is always something to be protected to avoid undesired consequences.)

- QUESTION: "My last dentist didn't take photos of my teeth so why do you need to take them?"
- ANSWER: "We take the photos so we have a complete set of records from which Dr. Jones will develop a plan that's best for you. Dr. Jones makes sure she has all the information she needs before beginning any type of treatment on her patients and the photos are a very important part."

- QUESTION: "Is there any way we can cut the cost for all this?"
- ANSWER: "I can check with the doctor. Which part don't you want to fix?"
  (Answer the question, then this is one of those times when you should shut up.)

"WILL MY INSURANCE COVER IT?"

Sound familiar? As a production dental assistant, you should be prepared to address this question. A lot of the time I hear this answered with "You'll have to ask the person at the front desk." or "Let me go ask the person at the front desk." If the "person at the front desk" knows the answer, why shouldn't you know it as well? You should. You should know the answer before you even begin the discussion about their treatment plan. I like to avoid using the words "dental insurance" because it's not really insurance at all. I prefer "dental benefits" because that's what it is. A dental benefits company will only pay up to their maximum per calendar year. The specific amount is an agreement between the patient and the company and you're just submitting it on their behalf. They won't pay more if the patient is in some sort of accident. In that case, any additional assistance would be provided by their auto insurance or workers' compensation-depending on the circumstances of how the injury occurred. Here's how I would address this question:

Patient: "Will my insurance cover it?"

Me: "Your dental benefits company will cover any amount up to your calendar year maximum. It looks like yours is $1500 per year so you will receive a $1500 discount off of your dental treatment for this year." (Then I would, of course, shut up.)

TAKING AN ACTIVE ROLE IN INCREASING PRACTICE PRODUCTION

How are you contributing to the financial success of the business? Take a look at the schedule and determine when you will have the opportunity to generate income. One example of how the dental assistant can help build practice production is to create value for accepting the treatment plan for a nightguard. Find the photos that were taken to document the damage at the last appointment, grab a hand-mirror for the patient and talk with them about it. Show them what changes have taken place since their last visit by pointing out how their front teeth have gotten shorter and the tips on their canines have become even more flattened. Tell a story of another patient who waited to get a nightguard to save money and ended up needing to spend more than twice as much to repair the damage as a result. Remind the patient that dental problems don't get any smaller and they don't get any cheaper. If you have successfully created value for a nightguard, you should be able to add about $600 to your daily production total. What's your production goal for the day? Not the practice goal. Your goal. I've been a part of many team meetings and huddles, as well as observed them over the years. It seems that the clinical staff mostly listens while the office manager and dentist talk about "where we're at on production". As a dental assistant assuming my role in treatment acceptance, I was just as responsible for generating income as anyone else in the office. Every Monday, we would meet up to write our production and collection totals from the previous week on the board next to our names. Our production was income we scheduled or "sold" and collection was any money we collected. A lot of the time, I (the dental assistant of all people) had the highest totals. I'll show and explain hypothetically how my portion of the income might be generated but basically we recorded the numbers next to our names on a table like the one below. Keep in mind that I worked at a very high-end cosmetic practice so the procedures and associated fees I've listed may be very different from your office. It's not the type of treatment or the amounts that matter. It's about recognizing the potential income that you can generate and creating a good plan for making it happen at *your* office. *Image 6*

TEAM MEMBER	MON	TUES	WEDS	THURS	WEEKLY TOTAL
DDS 1					
DDS 2					
MGR					
JEN	$9K/$4K	$24K/$12K	$2400/$1200	$1275/$975	$36,675/$18,175

Image 6

So looking at my sample production/collection numbers above, I would say the week probably went something like this:

MONDAY: Since Monday was usually a lab work day for me, I probably made five nightguards at $200 each. I learned how to make the nightguards myself rather than sending them out so I could claim the production AND save the office $1000 on the total lab bill. In the midst of my lab work, I may have answered the phone and scheduled a patient for an $8000 appointment to begin orthodontic treatment, collecting $4000 over the phone to reserve the time. See, it's only Monday and I'm already raking it in!
$9,000/$4,000

TUESDAY: These production/collection numbers might have been generated by a case presentation for 6-8 veneers that resulted in treatment acceptance and an appointment scheduled at a cost of $24,000. Hypothetically, I would have then walked to the front with the patient's credit card, swiped it for half the amount- $12,000- to secure the first appointment and brought the receipt back to the room for the patient to sign and receive their copy, along with the appointment card for their next visit. Notice that nobody else needed to get involved in this transaction, leaving my fellow team members available to assist other patients in person or on the phone to produce and collect income toward their own goals.
$24,000/$12,000

WEDNESDAY: These amounts could possibly be generated by a new patient consultation that resulted in an appointment scheduled in the amount of $2400 for them to come back for photos, impressions, x-rays, etc… and I would have collected half down- $1200 to set the appointment.
$2400/$1200

THURSDAY: A patient may have come in for a cleaning appointment and ended up accepting treatment for me to take check-up x-rays- $75, take impressions and a bite for a nightguard- $600 and set-up to do in-office whitening- $600 the same day they come on for their nightguard fitting/delivery. So I would have collected a total of $975 for the bite-wings, the nightguard records and half-down- $600 for the in-office whitening appointment

$1275/$975

The week I just described was likely very close to how I planned it so I could meet my goals, but then a hygiene patient randomly asked to set up a whitening appointment too so that was just luck. It's nice to have that kind of situation pop up so you can not only exceed your goal, but also to make up for any planned income that didn't happen. I always liked to have my daily goals written down to help motivate me and you might want to do the same thing.

SETTING YOUR OWN PRODUCTION GOALS

Not sure how to start? Try my way! Print a schedule, make some notes, set some goals and compare the two production totals. Quite a difference, isn't there? This is just an example of what I would do if this were my schedule for the day. This is all hypothetical, of course, but you get the idea. Remember that it's much easier to get treatment acceptance from patients that are already coming to your office than the new ones coming in. A lot of new patients are just shopping when they visit your office and may not be ready to buy from you just yet. Some of them will become patients and some won't and that's ok. It's important to get the new patients into your office but don't forget about the potential income that's already there. Just like in sales, people are more likely to buy a new product if they have already been doing business with you- when they *Believe, Like* and *Trust* you. There are those words again! So pay attention to the potential production that walks into your office every day. You have been (or should be) reminding them of their outstanding treatment plans whenever they come in. So like planes that are circling above the airport, waiting for clearance to come in, these patients will eventually have to land and you should be ready to welcome them at the gate and guide them to their next destination: treatment! *Image 7*

SCHEDULED PRODUCTION	YOUR NOTES	GOALS/POTENTIAL PRODUCTION
PROPHY, EXAM $175	1st pro/exam in 3 yrs- been living abroad	Take an FMX: $150
IN-OFFICE WHITENING $600	Pt has crown on #9, she knows it won't whiten but she really likes the shape-afraid to change it if it won't be the same	Start tx plan to replace crown by taking impressions for wax-up so pt can approve shape before prep appt: $1500
COMPOSITE #31 $295	#30 has a small occlusal pit alloy- would look better w/ resin	Replace the alloy on #30 while pt is numb: $295
BUCCAL CLASS IV FILL OUT #20 RE-DO $0	2nd time pt has awakened in morning and filling is gone	Take impressions and bite for a nightguard: $600
NP CONSULTATION $95	Pt wants veneers in time for daughter's wedding	Offer to do pt's dx records today: $1800
FX PORCELAIN- CROWN #3 $75	2nd crown pt's broken this year- he wants to know why	Take impressions, bite and facebow records for a bite analysis: $450
TOTAL: $1390	$1390? I can do better than that!	TOTAL: $5740

Image 7

Keep track of the income you generate for the business each year so you have the information when it's time to ask the boss for a raise. Unless you have a previous agreement, your employer is in no way obligated to give you a pay increase just because a year has passed.

Give the boss a reason to WANT to give you a raise!

"STORES ARE NEVER NICE TO PEOPLE; THEY'RE NICE TO CREDIT CARDS."

Do you remember that line from Pretty Woman? It applies here too. I've noticed how a dental assistant's attitude can turn sour when they have to work on a patient who is, well… difficult. I used to dread working on these patients until I realized how much a lot of these unpleasant customers spend on their dental treatment. It seems that some people are used to being treated like royalty and treating others like peasants. I had the opportunity to help treat some very affluent patients in my days of dental assisting. Some of them were absolutely delightful people who I really enjoyed helping because they appreciated me and treated me with respect. Then there were the ones who bitched about every little thing, bossed me around like I was a member of their household staff and were generally a complete pain in the ass to have in the office. But I was nice to their credit cards and you should be too. Don't let these high-maintenance patients and their socially inept ways keep you from reaching your production goals! Paste that smile on, resist the temptation to impale them with a sharp instrument and be nice to those credit cards!

Picture them with horns if you must, but be nice to their credit cards!

SOME MILLIONAIRES JUST PREFER OLD CARS AND CHEAP SHOES

And some ladies have a $10,000 handbag and an $8000 nose and will still haggle with you about a $1500 crown. You really never know and assumptions can be costly. There's the guy who drives up in what might be his first car; the one he bought with the money he earned delivering pizzas in high school. Could be he's wearing shoes he got in college and he probably graduated when Star Wars was still in theaters. That same guy might be ready to spend $50,000 on his teeth because that's how he wants to spend it. People spend their money on what THEY feel to be valuable. For some that might mean a fancy new car or a few weeks on a tropical island. For others it might be something really weird like one of those creepy antique doll collections. You never know so be careful not to make assumptions about how patients want to spend their money.

I've been a fly on a wall in a number of offices and have overheard many conversations pertaining to a certain patient coming in later that day. Much of the time, one team member will say that a certain patient is coming in and wonder aloud if they're ready to start a specific treatment plan yet. I've been shocked to hear that the response is something like "Oh don't ask him about it again. He never wants to do it." He will when he's ready.

I recently saw my hair stylist. She had left me two messages over the last few weeks to remind me that she had moved to a new location and that it was time to make an appointment to get my hair trimmed. I still hadn't gotten a chance to call her back when my phone rang at the exact time I was sitting at my desk with my calendar in front of me. I saw her number on the screen, answered and set up an appointment with her the following week. It was something I knew I needed to do but work and other obligations kept me from making it a priority. If she had given up and assumed I just didn't want to come to her new location and continue to see her for my hair care, she would have lost production. Her perseverance paid off and I scheduled the appointment because she happened to call when I happened to be ready. I know, sometimes you're not sure if you're being persistent or bothersome and the line between the two can be a fine one. If you're not sure, then find out. You can remind them of the treatment needed followed by a statement like "I don't mean to bug you about it, but I just want you to know that we're ready to take care of you when it's a good time for you to do it. I know how busy you are so you're often putting others' needs before your own. I just want to make sure you take care of you too!" Most people are going to be pleased that you're not only considering their other obligations, but also that you're acknowledging how hard they work to accommodate others and that will make them feel understood and appreciated; like at least someone knows how hard they work even if it's their dental assistant rather than their employer! Even if the patient doesn't schedule, you've made her feel good about the efforts she's making in other areas of her life. You want your patients to have positive thoughts as they drive back to work for the afternoon and maybe mention their good experience to a co-worker too!

IT'S JUST TOO MUCH

So the doctor had just laid out a comprehensive, multi-appointment treatment plan for our patient, explained each step and the fees associated with each portion. He then left the room so she and I could chat about it and I could hopefully guide her in the direction of setting up her first appointment to get started. As usual, I began the discussion with "So what do you think about all this?" She said "It's just too much." Well, I was thinking, the fees associated with this type of treatment plan aren't cheap- that's for sure. I'm glad I didn't say it out loud because that's not what she was talking about. It turns out that she wasn't the least bit concerned about the cost of treatment. She was talking about the composite the doctor had just temporarily placed over her front teeth. You might be familiar with an in-mouth preview that is sometimes called a mock-up. It helps to give the patient an idea of how their smile will look by the end of treatment- and this particular patient's mock-up was "just too much". So my job here was not to get the patient to accept the fees for the treatment as is often the case. She had already accepted the cost; I needed to sell the actual treatment! First I had to figure out which part was "just too much" so I asked. Her response didn't help much- "I don't know. It's just too much." Hmm, I had to be careful here not to say "Oh you mean this part?" about something else entirely. She could have been saying they were too white, too long, involved more teeth than she was expecting. I really wasn't sure. So I handed her the mirror and asked her to show me what she meant. Although at that point all she did was grimace and make a sort of claw out of her hand in front of her mouth, I finally figured out that she didn't like how thick her veneers would be and wasn't sure she wanted them if they would feel that weird. (Oh, that!) It was then easy for me to explain that we will take away just enough tooth structure to make room for her new smile design so it will feel natural and not be "too much".

IMPROVING DENTIST-ASSISTANT COMMUNICATION AND WORKING TOGETHER TO REACH YOUR GOALS

Having spent much of my professional life as a dental assistant, I know that getting your boss to communicate with you can sometimes be like... pulling teeth. If your boss is not a strong communicator, then you need to step up and voice how you would like to be more involved in treatment acceptance. Let the doctor know how you think you can help the office generate more production and unless they don't want to make more money, they'll probably listen. Some dentists have told me that they feel uncomfortable when chatting with patients about cosmetic dentistry- like they feel guilty for selling it to them- and I think patients sense that. Is that the case at your office? That's not going to help you reach your treatment acceptance goals so it might be a good idea for you to do something about it. Maybe the doctor can come in to greet the patient, provide the general information about the treatment planned, and then leave the room so you can talk with the patient about it. A "hand-off" I call it, and it's important that it's done smoothly. You never want the patient to feel abandoned by the dentist and left to speak with the assistant as if they had no choice. Here's an example of what I think is a good hand-off:

Dentist: *"Well, that's the plan I came up with for you. I'll let you and Jane talk about it together since she says I'm better at dentistry than I am at explaining things to my patients. (Keep it light, even humorous.) Do you have any other questions for me right now? No? Well, just send Jane to fetch me if you change your mind."*

Make sure the patient knows the dentist is still available. By available, I mean ready to pop back into the room in 10 seconds if the patient has an additional question; not 5 minutes later at a stopping point during an operative procedure in another room. Respect your patient by scheduling extra time during a case presentation appointment.

Dental assistant: *"OK, so I really think we've got a great plan for you but how do you feel about it?"*

An open-ended question at this point is very important and once you've asked, you guessed it! Shut up. Wait for the patient to answer. In a perfect world, the patient will say "I feel great about it! When can I get started?" But since that's not typically the case, you will need to be in tune with what your patient might be thinking or feeling and get acquainted with their psychology. They don't teach that in dental assisting school, do they?

BECOMING MORE KNOWLEDGEABLE ABOUT HUMAN BEHAVIOR AND HOW WE MAKE DECISIONS

I credit much of my patient communication skills to my "Guest Service" training while working for The Walt Disney Company. Disney makes it their business to know their customers' wants, needs, perceptions and emotions. They call this process their "Guestology". This makes it much easier for them to cater to the people who visit their theme parks, hotels and stores. You can gather the same information about your patients and make it much easier to give them the experience they're hoping for when they visit your office. If you meet or exceed their expectations, they may decide to complete their dental treatment at your office. There are other factors that might influence their decision making such as **past experiences, biases and escalation of commitment**- like when the investment of money becomes involved.

Past experiences may include a "bad experience" at the dentist. Do your best to find this out about the patient when you're getting to know them so you're aware of any such experience right from the beginning. If a patient may be reluctant to move forward with their treatment because they're afraid, special care should be taken during the case presentation to provide ongoing reassurance that you're aware of their past experience.

We've all been afraid at one time or another so now is a good time to tell a story of when you've been afraid to have a type of procedure. I like to tell the one about having my vision laser-corrected. Yes, I was afraid but I went through with the procedure and I'm so happy with the results! Let them know you understand how they feel. Understand. Remember that word. Patients want to know that you understand because understanding is associated with compassion. Your compassion and understanding will make them feel safer in your care despite their fear.

Time and again, I've heard clinical team members tell a patient "Oh don't worry, you'll be fine." often accompanied by a somewhat condescending hand-pat. Just because you think getting a couple fillings is no big deal, doesn't mean the patient isn't imagining the lunatic dentist scene from Marathon Man. Let the patient decide how they feel about it or they will only feel judged for being afraid which may lessen their trust in you.

That brings up another point- judging a patient for wanting to take a sedative to help them relax before and during their treatment. Again, "don't worry about it" with a hand-pat isn't going to calm the patient. Ultimately, it's up to the doctor, but I do recommend offering it as an option if they think it will make them feel more comfortable during their treatment. This will give them an added cushion of security as they face their fear which will make them even more likely to accept a treatment plan- the whole point of this little book.

Oh don't worry.
You'll be just fine.

Cognitive factors are circumstances or influences –rather than evidence- that contribute to the decision making process. I'm no psychologist, so the best way I can relate to this, without all the fancy schmancy terms, is to think of the young patient who is afraid of "getting a shot" for the first time. Most often, one of the parents has influenced the patient in such a way that the child has already decided that it's going to hurt.

Another situation that comes to mind would be a patient's first exam appointment at your office. The patient may come into that visit feeling a little defensive because their co-worker, who referred them, needed several fillings and told the patient the dentist might make them come back for "a bunch of fillings" too.

We need to be aware of these types of bias so we can still meet our goals. Sometimes it's calming the child of moronic parents who scare the bejeezus out of their kid before leaving him to have "sleepy juice dripped next to their tooth". Or it may be simply assuring a new patient that not everyone needs that many fillings (or any at all) and that the dentist won't know until she takes a look so let's wait and see before we worry about that! Whatever the bias, our goal is to work around it to achieve our desired outcome- treatment acceptance.

Escalation of commitment is another decision-making factor and probably the most predictable. There are situations we can all recall when the escalation of commitment briskly shuts down the treatment acceptance process. This of course, relates to money.

You're not sure what happened. The patient was so excited about getting a new smile and fixing the teeth that had been bothering him for so long. Next thing you know, he's walking out the door- without an appointment. This is why I prefer to talk with the patient about everything in the clinical area and why I think the assistant should be a big part of that. Remember, we're the ones who have the non-threatening relationship with the patient so I think the assistant should be empowered to have the financial discussion as well. Otherwise, you walk the patient up front to the "money-taker", who they may not know very well, and hope for the best. If I'm taking an active role in treatment acceptance and making money for this business, I would want more control over that outcome.

"BESIDES WHAT YOU SEE, I HAVE CONFIDENCE IN ME!"

Yeah, I know you're a dental professional, not Fraulein Maria from The Sound of Music. My point is that she was nervous in the beginning and apparently gained her confidence by singing and dancing all the way to the front gate of the Von Trapp's house to start her first day of work. Not to spoil it for you if you've not yet seen the musical, but she did end up winning over everyone she met on the other side of that fence. She built up her confidence and succeeded and you can too. The singing and dancing part is optional. I didn't know how to talk with patients about treatment acceptance and I certainly wasn't confident when

I began my career in dental assisting in 1994. I've been an intern, a new-hire, dropped instruments, broken stone models, had provisional crowns fall off, taken bad impressions, snapped a useless set of patient photos, put my foot in my mouth all the way up to my knee, cried all the way home after work- and in the shower before work. You name it; my confidence has been shaken like a can of pennies rattled at a disobedient puppy. Yet somehow, over the years I've learned how to teach the very skills that used to be such struggles for me. Ok, I still put my foot in my mouth sometimes; but only up to my ankle! Like learning how to take good impressions, it takes time to gain the confidence needed to feel comfortable guiding a patient toward treatment acceptance. Nothing has made me more confident than my time spent attending continuing education courses, reading dental journals and books and asking questions. So if you're lost, don't be afraid to ask for directions!

SCHOOLHOUSE ROCK WASN'T KIDDING! KNOWLEDGE REALLY IS POWER!

Power and money. Remember, we're caregivers but you're also running a business and (say it with me) the success of the business will be dependent upon its ability to consistently make money. Treatment acceptance means the patient is buying what you're selling and the more you know about what you're selling the better chance you'll have at selling it. So study up! Take a continuing education course whenever given the opportunity- even if you have to attend the class on your day off. Read articles and books in your spare time to learn more about new materials and techniques. Study dental business journals to keep a pulse on the financial concerns dentists are facing and become more educated on how you might be able to help ease the stress on your employer by doing your part to generate revenue for the business- and for you! Learn more about comprehensive dentistry so you can have more educated conversations with your patients as you guide them toward case acceptance for treatment plans that may involve such complex issues as vertical dimension. You don't need to tackle all the books and continuing education courses at once. Study the different procedures and reason for them as they come up on treatment plans. If you see that the doctor has planned a certain appointment type, make sure you learn everything you can about it so you'll be ready to confidently discuss it with the patient.

SO THERE YOU HAVE IT!

You've got a plan to help you contribute to the financial success of your employer; and that success will trickle down to you too! You're a confident, productive dental assistant! You're not just clinically talented; you can create value for the services offered to your patients. You know how to educate yourself about even the most complex treatment plans by using the resources all around you. You're tuned in to your patients' psyche and have the verbal skills you need to communicate with them effectively. You know how to set, meet and exceed your production goals. You're a dental assistant with a business edge, I'd say! Now get your smart, talented, confident self out there and play your role in treatment acceptance!

PLANNING TOOLS TO HELP YOU GET STARTED

1. List the services offered at your business and ways you can create value for each one.

2. Review the planned production for a daily schedule and look for ways you can generate more revenue.

3. Are there any skills you would like to learn that could help you become more valuable to your employer?

4. List ways you can gain the knowledge you need to help you reach your goals?

5. Discuss your new goals with your employer and find out how you might be rewarded for your efforts. Bonus program? Higher salary? Gift cards for restaurants, day spas or other leisure?

FOR DENTAL ASSISTANTS WHO ARE
REGISTERED IN THE STATE OF CALIFORNIA:

EARN 1 UNIT OF CONTINUING EDUCATION CREDIT
BY EMAILING YOUR FULL NAME
AND ANSWER TO #3,
TO:
jengreen@impressionsf.com

YOUR CONTINUING EDUCATION CREDITS WILL BE
ATTACHED IN A RETURN EMAIL TO YOU FOR PRINTING
OR TO SIMPLY SAVE FOR YOUR RECORDS.

www.ingramcontent.com/pod-product-compliance
Lightning Source LLC
Chambersburg PA
CBHW021852170526
45157CB00006B/2418